Sunshine

Pupil's Book 3

Englisch ab Klasse 1

AF202583

Erarbeitet von
Tanja Beattie (Ebersberg)
Stefanie Keller (Konstanz)
Nadine Kerler (Ulm)
Daniela Röbers (Erkelenz)
Caroline Schröder (München)
Gertrud Steinhausen (Ratingen)

Auf der Grundlage der Ausgabe von
Birgit Hollbrügge
und Ulrike Kraaz

Cornelsen

Contents

Symbols

listen to your partner or teacher

read

talk

play

listen to the CD, track 2

extra

draw or write

explain the rules / task in German

Hello again!

1 Talk about the picture.

I can see …

2 Read the words: *cowboy, football, hamburger, laptop, skateboard.*
Find the pictures.

3 Make a poster. Think. Pair. Share.

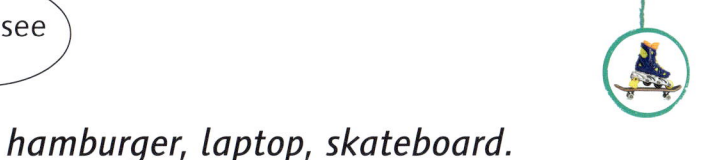

1 Listen to the rhyme. Point to the pictures.

2 Say the rhyme with a partner. Do the actions.

> 1, 2,
> how are you?

> 3, 4,
> touch the floor.

> 5, 6,
> no more tricks.

> 7, 8,
> don't be late.

> 9, 10,
> start again.

> 11, 12,
> say it yourself.

⭐ Do you know more numbers?
Say the numbers. Write the numbers. Work with a partner.

Meeting friends

🇬🇧 **Note**

Auf dem Bild siehst du eine Straße in England. Was fällt dir auf?

1 Talk about the picture.

⭐ What do you know about England? Think. Pair. Share.

2 Listen to your teacher. Point to the numbers. Say the colours.

3 Listen. Where do they live?

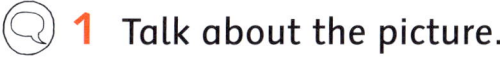

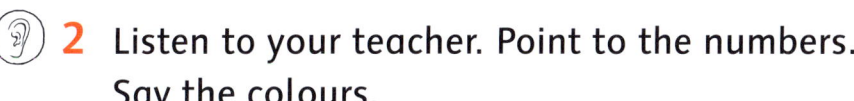
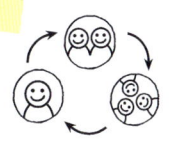

Door number 3 is yellow.

Number … is Harry's house.

1 Read the dialogue. Talk to a partner.

> Let's play Hopscotch!

> Good idea!

> Let's write the numbers in different colours.

> Can I have green? My favourite colour is green.

2 Listen. Point to the numbers.

3 Say the numbers.

4 Play 'Hopscotch'.

5 Explain.

> You start, Emily.

1

> 1, 2, …

> Good, Emily.

> 10, 9, 8, …

> Oops!

2

3

1 Talk about Harry's family.

This is …

2 Listen. Point to the pictures.

Let's talk

3 Read the dialogue. Talk to a partner.
⭐ More: Make up your own dialogue.

Have you got a sister?

No, I haven't. I've got a brother.

What's his name?

His name is Pete.

More to explore: **Colours and flags**

1 Look at the map. Where do they speak English?

Talk about the colours and the flags.

⭐ Listen to your partner. Point to the country.

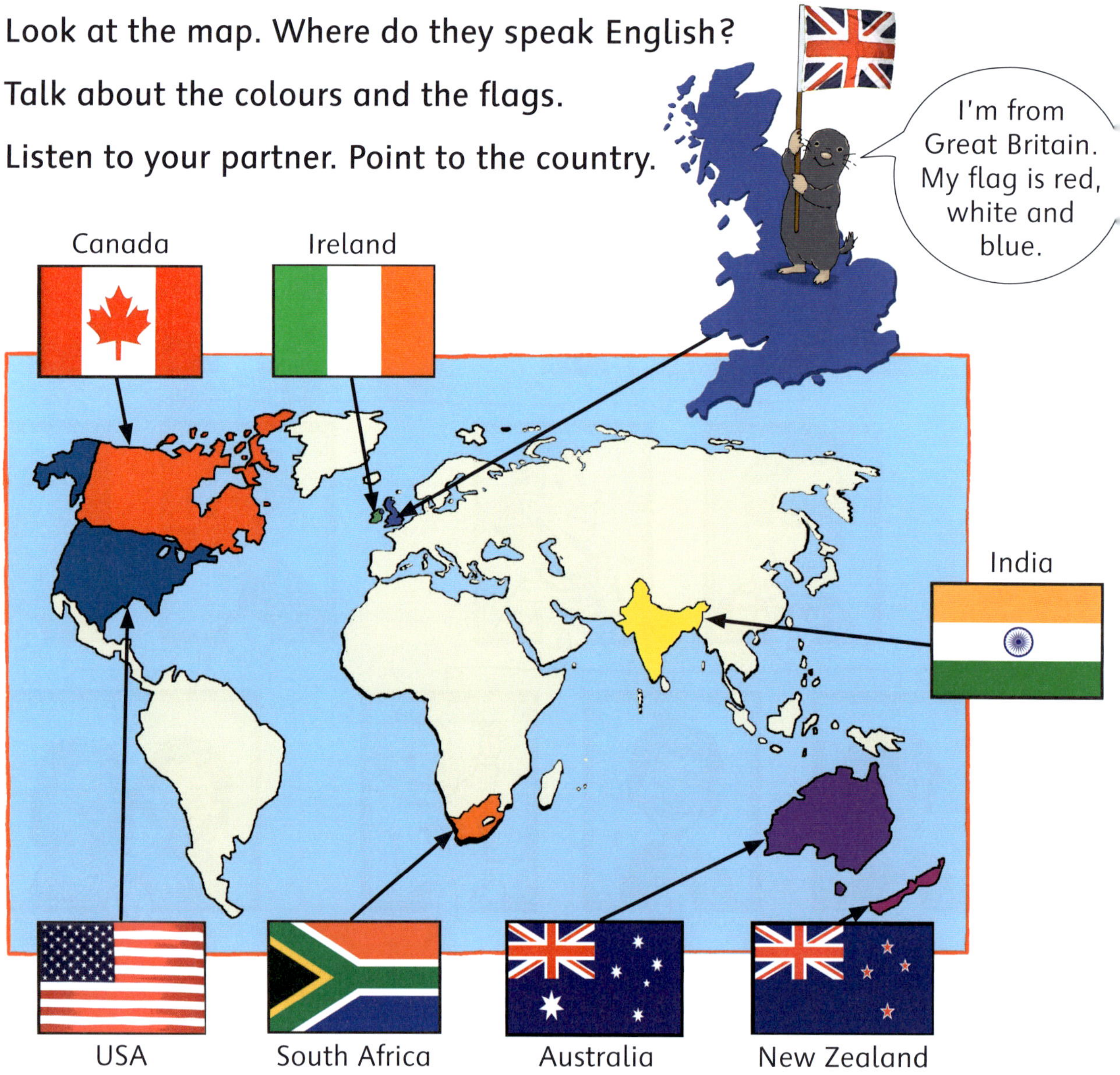

> I'm from Great Britain. My flag is red, white and blue.

Canada

Ireland

India

USA

South Africa

Australia

New Zealand

⭐ **What about you?**

> I live in Great Britain. My family is from …

> I live in Germany. My family is from …

1 Listen. Who is on the telephone?

> Hi, ...!

Let's talk

2 Read the dialogue. Talk to a partner.
⭐ More: Make up your own dialogue.

> Hi Lisa.

> Hi, Leon.

> Can you come and play?

> Yes, I can.

> OK. See you. Bye.

> See you. Bye-bye.

2

1 Talk about the picture. What pets can you see?

I can see …

2 Listen. What pets do the children have?

⭐ Read with a partner. What food do the pets like?

Rabbits like carrots.

I like apples.

Rabbits don't like popcorn.

I like dog food.

Story: **Rabbit's party**

1 Read the story.

2 Act out the story.

⭐ Read the party invitation.

Dear ...,
can you come to my party?

Yes, thank you. ☐
No, I'm sorry. ☐

From ...

Can you come to my party?

Yes, I can. Thank you.

Come in, please.

Thank you.

Thank you.

Mm, a hamster, a rat and a guinea pig. I like guinea pigs!

Mm, peanuts, carrots, apples – and lettuce. I like lettuce.

I like apples.

I like peanuts.

Let's have a party. Come on, let's eat and drink!

Dog, come in!

Great trick!

 1 Read the words and sentences.

 **2** Explain.

 **3** Play the game.

Go to the
matching
picture.

Miss
a turn.

START

dog

rabbit

Go to the
matching
word.

Take a card.
Say a
sentence.

apple

rat

cat

carrot

hamster

lettuce

guinea pig

peanuts

FINISH

More to explore: **Dogs**

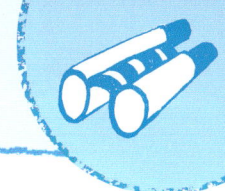

 1 Listen. Point to the pictures.

sheep dog

rescue dog

police dog

guide dog

2 Read the speech bubbles with a partner.

3 Do the dog actions with your partner. Guess the actions. Take turns.

4 Play the game with your class.

5 Explain.

I'm sleepy.

I'm scared.

I'm happy.

I'm sad.

I want to play!

I'm hungry.

Watch the film.

 1 Talk about the picture. Where's Mr Mole?

 **2** Listen to the song. Point to the school things in the picture.

📖 ⭐ Read the text with a partner.

✏️ ⭐ Where are the school things?
Write sentences: *The rubber is on the table.*

Think. Pair. Share.

Where's Mr Mole?
Where can he be?
Where's Mr Mole?
Let me see.

Is he in the school bag?
Is he on the book?
Or under the table?
Let's have a look.

No! Not there!

🇬🇧 **Note**

In vielen Klassen in Großbritannien gibt es einen zweiten Lehrer oder eine zweite Lehrerin. Diese Person nennt man *classroom assistant*.

1 Read the texts.

 2 Explain.

 3 Play the game in groups of 4.

① Take 5 cards from your word box.

② Put your cards on the table.

③ Shuffle all the cards.

④ Give 5 cards to each player.

⑤ Ask questions.

Can I have the pencil, please?

Here you are.

Have you got a ruler, please?

Sorry, I haven't got a ruler.

The player with the most cards wins.

Story: **Jack's bad day**

1 Listen to the story.

2 Read the story.

3 What happens in the end?
Think. Pair. Share.

⭐ Act out the story.

> Read the text.

> That's my book. Give it back, Jack!

①

②

> Draw an apple.

③

> That's my pencil. Give it back, Jack!

④

> Colour the apple red.

⑤

> That's my felt tip. Give it back, Jack!

⑥

> It's time for lunch.

⑦

⑧

?

3

More to explore: **School in Britain**

1 Talk about the pictures.

2 Listen. Point to the pictures.

3 Read the texts.

 **Note**

In England schaust du zuerst nach rechts, wenn du eine Straße überquerst. Weißt du warum?

A **lollipop man** helps children cross the road.

Some children walk to school with the **walking bus**.

This is a **school building**.

School starts with **assembly**.

4 Make a school badge. You need:

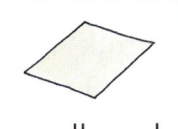				
cardboard	felt tips or coloured pencils	scissors	a safety pin	sticky tape

① Draw a circle on the cardboard.
Write your school's name.
Colour the badge.

② Cut out the badge.

③ Tape a safety pin to the back of your badge.

Watch the film.

5 Explain.

What I can do and say

A word web

family

brother
mother
father
sister

This is my ...
I've got a ...
I haven't got a ...

aunt, grandfather, uncle ...   How many ... have you got?

Make your own word web

Think. Pair. Share.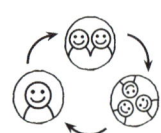

school

pets

friends and family

My name is ... · This is my ... ·
It's a ... · It likes ... ·
What colour is ... / do you like? ·
Its name is ... · I'm ... ·
What about you? · Where are
you from? · I'm from ... ·
I'm in class ... · My teacher
is ... · Can I have ..., please? ·
Here you are. · Thanks. ·
You're welcome. ·
My favourite ...

What can you do or say in English? Think!

I can ...

 ... say the words.

... write the words.

... ask and answer questions.

What do you want to be better at?

What I can do and say

You can find more words

- in your Pupil's Book.

- in your Activity Book.

- in a dictionary.

- on the Internet.

Play 'Pick a pair' with your mini picture cards.

Game for 2 players. You need: 2 sets of mini picture cards

(1) Put the cards on the table.

A dog!

(2) Pick 2 cards. Turn them over. Name the cards.

It's a pair!

(3) 2 cards the same? Keep the pair and play again.

My turn!

(4) Not the same? Put them back again.

The player with the most cards wins.

4 The second-hand shop

Note

| jeans | – Jeans |
| T-shirt | – T-Shirt |

1 Talk about the picture.

I can see ...

2 Listen to your partner.
Find the clothes in the picture.

3 What's in the shop? Write. *There's ... / There are ...*

⭐ Play 'I spy'.

| cap | dress | gloves | hat | jacket | pullover | sandals |
| scarf | shirt | skirt | shoes | socks | trousers | T-shirt |

Do you like my coat?

1 Listen to your teacher. Who is it?

2 Choose one child. Talk to a partner.

⭐ Write.

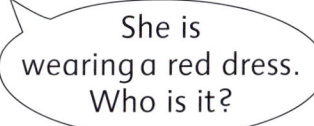

She is wearing a red dress. Who is it?

It's …

Note

she = girl

he = boy

①	②	③
Sarah	Harry	Kate

④	⑤	⑥
Samir	Emily	John

Let's talk

1 Read the dialogue. Talk to a partner.
⭐ More: Make up your own dialogue.

2 Talk to your partner. Ask: *Do you like the ...?*

1 Read the story.

2 Act out the story.

Story: **The smartest giant in town**

 1 Listen to the story. Point to the pictures.

 2 Talk about the pictures. How does the story end?

 ⭐ Read the rhyme with a partner.

Find the matching pictures.

What about picture 6?

> My tie is a scarf for a cold giraffe.
>
> My shirt's on a boat as a sail for a goat.
>
> My shoe is a house for a little white mouse.
>
> One of my socks is a bed for a fox.
>
> My belt helped a dog who was crossing a bog.

Note

Find the rhyming words.
boat – goat
…
Make a list.

More to explore: **School uniforms**

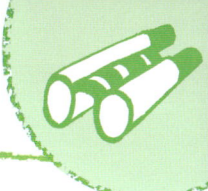

1 Talk about school uniforms. What is the boy wearing?
What is the girl wearing? Say: *The girl is wearing …*

a cardigan · a pullover · a shirt · shoes · a skirt · socks · a tie · trousers

 **Note**

In Großbritannien tragen die Kinder Uniformen in der Schule.
Wie findest du das?
Begründe!

⭐ Make your own school uniform. Think. Pair. Share.

2 Listen. Point to the pictures.

⭐ Listen to your partner. What school is it?

①

②

③

Watch the film.

| Queen's School | Swanage School | Blake School |

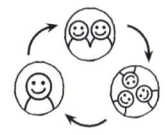

 4 Fächerübergreifendes Lernen: „Arts and crafts", s. HRU, S.283-286

twenty-five **25**

5 Free-time activities

1 Talk about the pictures.

2 Listen to the song. Point to the pictures.

3 Sing the song.

Football, music, books, TV
Bikes and comics, friends, PC
Tell me, tell me,
What about you?
Do you like the things I do?

Playing football
Is what I like
Watching TV
Riding my bike.

Listening to music
Tapping my feet
Meeting friends
In the street.

Reading books
And comics, too
Playing computer games.
What about you?

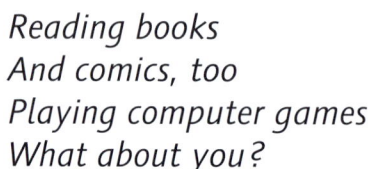

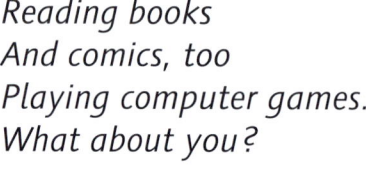

I like meeting friends. What do you like?

Let's talk

1 Read the dialogue. Talk to a partner.
⭐ More: Make up your own dialogue.

 2 Listen to the rhyme. Point to the pictures.

 3 Read the rhyme.

 ⭐ Make up a new rhyme. *Is it in …?*

Think. Pair. Share.

Words for your rhyme:

painting the wall ·
playing ball ·
garden shed · toilet

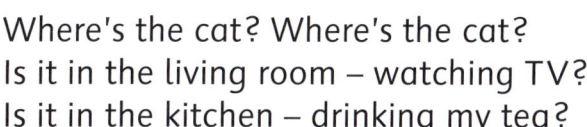

Where's the cat? Where's the cat?
Is it in the living room – watching TV?
Is it in the kitchen – drinking my tea?

Where's the cat? Where's the cat?
Is it in the bedroom – eating my shoe?
Is it in the bathroom – playing with shampoo?

Where's the cat? Where's the cat?
There it is – sleeping in Mum's favourite hat.

1 Look at the pictures. Where's Harry/Kate/...?

2 Listen to your partner. Find the things in the pictures.

⭐ Write sentences. *There's* ... Look at your word list (page 41-44).

①

②

Story: **The babysitters**

48 **1** Listen to the story.
Point to the pictures.

2 Read the story.

1 Oh, this is boring.

2 Here's a great CD.

I don't like listening to music.

3 What about playing football?

Great idea! Where's my football?

Is your football in your bedroom?

4 No, it isn't in my bedroom.

Not in the living room, Nick!

Oh dear. Sorry!

5

48 **3** Listen to the story. What don't they say?

1 What about meeting friends?

2 What about playing computer games?

3 What about watching TV?

More to explore: **Rhymes and playground games**

 **1** Look at the pictures.
Read the names of the games.

2 Talk about the games.

3 Listen. Point to the pictures.

Playground games:

connect 4 · hide and seek · skipping · tag

 4 Read the rules.

 5 Explain.

 6 Play 'Rock, paper, scissors'.

Note

Was spielst du gerne auf dem Schulhof? Vergleiche.

① Say and do.

Rock, paper, scissors. Show!

② Who's the winner?

rock

paper   scissors

③ Two hands the same?

Play again!

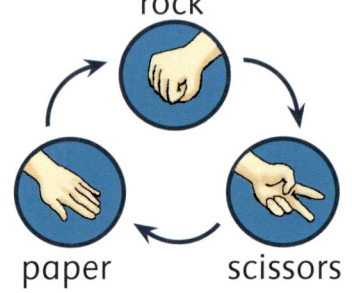

Fächerübergreifendes Lernen: „P.E. (Sports)", s. HRU, S. 287–288

In the park

1 Talk about the picture. Where is Mr Mole?

2 Listen to your teacher. Find the numbers.

⭐ Talk to a partner.
How many dogs / tables / scooters / … can you see?

⭐ What do you like doing in the park? Make a list.

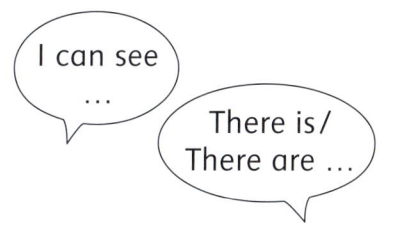

I can see …

There is /
There are …

1 Talk about the picture.

2 Listen. What does the boy say?

⭐ Write a shopping list.

How much is …?

It's …

My shopping list
1 apple

Let's talk

3 Read the dialogue. Talk to a partner.

⭐ More: Make up your own dialogue.

Hi, can I help you?

I'd like a strawberry special. How much is it?

It's £ 1.50. Anything else?

No, thank you. That is all.

Story: **Where's my ice cream?**

1 Listen to the story.

2 Read the speech bubbles.

3 Say what's right and what's wrong.

 **1** Look at the signs. Read the sentences. Match.

2 Talk about the signs.

 Draw a park sign. Write. Think. Pair. Share.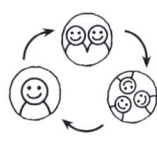

Wheelchair access.

No ball games.

Please keep off the grass.

No bikes.

No horse riding.

Can you dig holes in the park?

No dogs.

Watch the film.

1 Talk about the picture.

2 Whose birthday is it today? Sing the song.

3 Listen to the song. Point to the pictures.

Someone's birthday is today, is today, is today.
Someone's birthday is today, and it's our ...

Let's prepare a birthday cake,
Birthday cake, birthday cake.
Let's prepare a birthday cake,
Just for our ...

Add a candle for each year,
For each year, for each year.
Add a candle for each year,
Just for our ...

Make a special birthday card,
Birthday card, birthday card.
Make a special birthday card,
Just for our ...

 **Note**

Zum Geburtstag tragen englische Kinder gerne selbst gebastelte Hüte oder Kronen. Wie feierst du deinen Geburtstag?

Happy Birthday!

Special days: **Christmas**

1 Which Christmas words do you know?

Think. Pair. Share.

 **Note**

Kinder in Großbritannien hängen am 24.12. Strümpfe auf.
Diese werden über Nacht gefüllt. Kennst du weitere Besonderheiten?

2 Talk about the picture.

3 Look at the pictures. Find the Christmas things in the house.

⭐ Find more Christmas things in the house.

Special days: **Valentine's Day**

1 Read the card.

Note

When is Valentine's Day?
Who was Saint Valentine?
Find out more.

Moles are cool

Moles are clever

I will love you

forever and ever

From **?**

2 Read the story with a partner.

⭐ Present it in class.

The world's smallest Valentine

It's Valentine's Day.
Olivia is visiting her granddad
and grandma.

Olivia: This is for you, Granddad.
Granddad: Oh, thank you. What is it?
Olivia: It's a Valentine card.
Granddad: What's inside the card?
Olivia: A tomato seed.
Granddad: A tomato seed?
Olivia: Yes. The old name for tomato is 'love apple'.
Granddad: Thank you, Olivia. A love apple seed.
What a lovely Valentine!

1 Make your own Easter bunny.

You need:

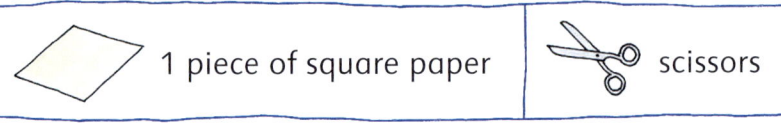

| | 1 piece of square paper | | scissors |

Fold and cut the paper.

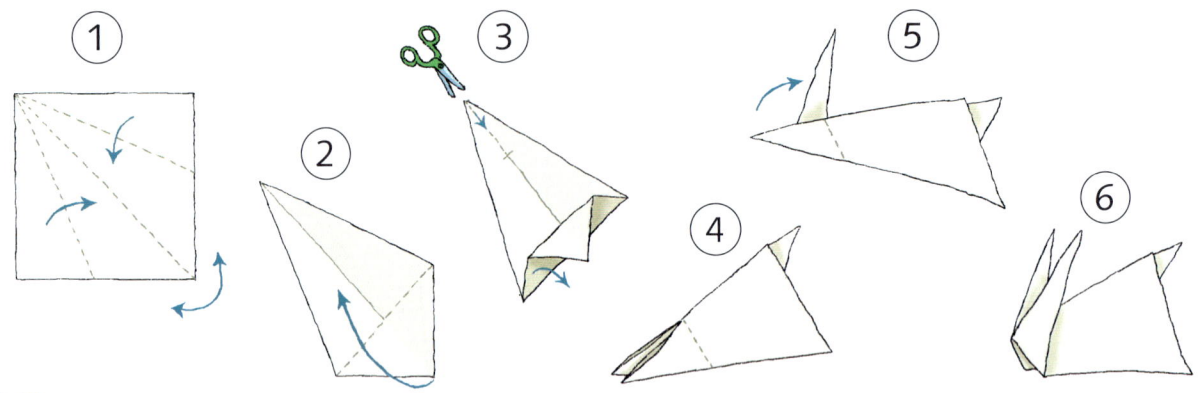

2 Explain.

3 Listen to the Easter rhyme.

4 Say the rhyme.

Here's a bunny.
With ears so funny,
And here is his hole in the ground.
And when a noise he hears,
He pricks up his ears,
And hops in his hole in the ground.

What I can do and say

A word web

dress	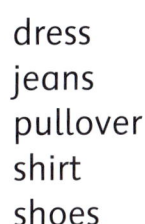	Do you like …?
jeans		Yes, I do.
pullover		No, I don't.
shirt		I like …
shoes		I don't like …
		I'm …

cold …   How many … have you got?

Make your own word web. Think. Pair. Share.

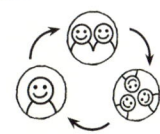

hobbies   **special days**

fruit and drinks

Can I help you? · Yes, please. · No, thank you. · I'd like … · Can I have … please? · Here you are. · You're welcome. · How much is …? · How many …? · Please come to my party. · Can you come to my party? · Yes, I can. · No, thank you. · I'm sorry. · That's OK. · What about you? · Merry Christmas! · Happy Birthday!

What can you do or say in English? Think!

I can …

(○) … say the words.

(✎) … write the words.

(○) … ask and answer questions.

What do you want to be better at?

What I can do and say

Can you write the word?

books

(1) Read the word.

(2) Look up.

(3) Look at the word again.

(4) Write down the word.

(5) Check the word.

Play 'Bingo'. with your mini picture cards.

Game for 3 or more (1 caller).
You need: 2 sets of mini picture cards for each player.

How to play:

Mouse!

Bingo!

(1) Put down 6 or 9 cards.

(2) Listen to the caller. Have you got the card? Turn it over. Listen again.

(3) Have you got all cards? You are the winner.

Word list

A

apple Apfel
aunt Tante

B

banana Banane
bedroom Schlafzimmer
behind hinter
big groß
birthday Geburtstag
birthday cake Geburtstagskuchen
birthday card Geburtstagskarte
birthday present Geburtstagsgeschenk
black schwarz
blackboard Tafel
blue blau
book Buch
boots Stiefel
boring langweilig
boy Junge
bread Brot
brother Bruder
brown braun
budgie Wellensittich
bye tschüss

C

can können
candle Kerze
carrot Möhre
cat Katze
chair Stuhl
cherry Kirsche
chocolate Schokolade
Christmas Weihnachten
Christmas Day Weihnachtstag (25.12.)
Christmas Eve Heiligabend (24.12.)
Christmas tree Weihnachtsbaum
class Klasse
classroom Klassenzimmer
coat Mantel
cold kalt
colour Farbe, ausmalen
come kommen
cousin Cousin(e)

D

dog Hund
draw zeichnen
dress Kleid, ankleiden
drink Getränk, trinken

E

Easter Ostern
Easter basket Osterkorb
Easter bunny Osterhase
Easter egg Osterei
eat essen
eight acht
eighty achtzig

F

family Familie
father Vater
Father Christmas Weihnachtsmann
favourite Lieblings-
felt tip Filzstift
fifty fünfzig
fish Fisch
five fünf
food Essen
football Fußball
forty vierzig
four vier
frog Frosch
fruit Obst

G

garden shed Gartenhaus
girl Mädchen
gloves Handschuhe
glue stick Klebstift
good gut
great toll
green grün
grey grau
guinea pig Meerschweinchen

H

hamster Hamster
happy glücklich
hat Mütze
helmet (Fahrrad-)Helm
house Haus

I

ice cream Eiscreme
in in
in front of vor
in-line skates Inlineskates

J

jacket Jacke
juice Saft

Word list

L

lemon Zitrone
lettuce (Kopf-) Salat
like mögen
listening to music Musik hören
living room Wohnzimmer
lunch Mittagessen
lunch box Brotdose

M

meeting friends Freunde treffen
Merry Christmas!
   Frohe Weihnachten!
milk Milch
mother Mutter
mouse Maus

N

next to neben
nine neun
ninety neunzig
number Zahl

O

on auf
one eins
orange orange, Apfelsine

P

peach Pfirsich
peanuts Erdnüsse
pen Füller
pencil Bleistift
pencil case Federmappe
pencil sharpener Bleistiftspitzer
pet Haustier
pink rosa
play spielen
playing computer games
   Computerspiele spielen
playing football Fußball spielen
plum Pflaume
pound (£) Pfund (britisches Geld)
pullover Pullover

R

rabbit Kaninchen
rat Ratte
read lesen
red rot
reindeer Rentier
riding my bike Fahrrad fahren
room Zimmer

rope skipping Seilspringen
rubber Radiergummi
ruler Lineal

S

sandals Sandalen
scarf Schal
school Schule
school bag Schultasche
school bus Schulbus
scissors Schere
scooter Roller
seven sieben
seventy siebzig
shirt Hemd
shoes Schuhe
shop Laden
sister Schwester
six sechs
sixty sechzig
skirt Rock
small klein
socks Socken
stocking Strumpf
strawberry Erdbeere
swimsuit Badeanzug

T

teacher Lehrer, Lehrerin
telephone number Telefonnummer
ten zehn
thirty dreißig
three drei
tomato Tomate
trousers Hose
twenty zwanzig
twins Zwillinge
two zwei

U

uncle Onkel
under unter

V

very sehr

W

watching TV fernsehen
white weiß

Y

yellow gelb

A

acht   eight
achtzig   eighty
ankleiden   dress
Apfel   apple
Apfelsine   orange
auf   on
ausmalen   colour

B

Badeanzug   swimsuit
Banane   banana
blau   blue
Bleistift   pencil
Bleistiftspitzer   pencil sharpener
braun   brown
Brot   bread
Brotdose   lunch box
Bruder   brother
Buch   book

C

Computerspiele spielen
   playing computer games
Cousin(e)   cousin

D

drei   three
dreißig   thirty

E

eins   one
Eiscreme   ice cream
Erdbeere   strawberry
Erdnüsse   peanuts
essen, Essen   eat, food

F

Fahrrad fahren   riding a bike
Familie   family
Farbe   colour
Federmappe   pencil case
fernsehen   watching TV
Filzstift   felt tip
Fisch   fish
Freunde treffen   meeting friends
Frohe Weihnachten!   Merry Christmas!
Frosch   frog
Füller   pen
fünf   five
fünfzig   fifty
Fußball   football
Fußball spielen   playing football

G

Gartenhaus   garden shed
Geburtstag   birthday
Geburtstagsgeschenk   birthday present
Geburtstagskarte   birthday card
Geburtstagskuchen   birthday cake
gelb   yellow
Getränk   drink
glücklich   happy
grau   grey
groß   big
grün   green
gut   good

H

Hamster   hamster
Handschuhe   gloves
Haus   house
Haustier   pet
Heiligabend (24.12.)   Christmas Eve
Helm (Fahrrad-)   helmet
Hemd   shirt
hinter   behind
Hose   trousers
Hund   dog
hundert   hundred

I

in   in
Inlineskates   in-line skates

J

Jacke   jacket
Junge   boy

K

kalt   cold
Kaninchen   rabbit
Katze   cat
Kerze   candle
Kirsche   cherry
Klasse   class
Klassenzimmer   classroom
Klebestift   glue stick
Kleid   dress
klein   small
kommen   come
können   can

L

Laden   shop
langweilig   boring
Lehrer, Lehrerin   teacher

Word list

lesen read
Lieblings- favourite
Lineal ruler

M

Mädchen girl
Mantel coat
Maus mouse
Meerschweinchen guinea pig
Milch milk
Mittagessen lunch
mögen like
Möhre carrot
Musik hören listening to music
Mutter mother
Mütze hat

N

neben next to
neun nine
neunzig ninety

O

Obst fruit
Onkel uncle
Orange, orange orange
Osterei Easter egg
Osterhase Easter bunny
Osterkorb Easter basket
Ostern Easter

P

Pfirsich peach
Pflaume plum
Pfund (£) pound
Pullover pullover

R

Radiergummi rubber
Ratte rat
Rentier reindeer
Rock skirt
Roller scooter
rosa pink
rot red

S

Saft juice
(Kopf-) Salat lettuce
Sandals Sandalen
Schal scarf
Schere scissors
Schlafzimmer bedroom
Schokolade chocolate

Schuhe shoes
Schulbus school bus
Schule school
Schultasche school bag
schwarz black
Schwester sister
sechs six
sechzig sixty
sehr very
Seilspringen rope skipping
sieben seven
siebzig seventy
Socken socks
spielen play
Stiefel boots
Strumpf stocking
Stuhl chair

T

Tafel blackboard
Tante aunt
Telefonnummer telephone number
toll great
Tomate tomato
trinken drink
tschüss bye

U

unter under

V

Vater father
vier four
vierzig forty
vor in front of

W

Weihnachten Christmas
Weihnachtsbaum Christmas tree
Weihnachtsmann Father Christmas
Weihnachtstag (25.12.) Christmas Day
weiß white
Wellensittich budgie
Wohnzimmer living room

Z

Zahl number
zehn ten
zeichnen draw
Zimmer room
Zitrone lemon
zwanzig twenty
zwei two